Bright Start Right Start

Words

seashell

apple

Jim Bear

tiger

road roller

thirty

Betty Bear

Scribblers
S
Bright Start Right Start

A world of words for a brighter start

hair
forehead
eyebrow
eye
face
ear
cheek
nose
mouth
lip
chin
neck
shoulder
arm
hand
ball
elbow
boy

Contents

Betty Bear

What colour is the polar bear?

How to use this book

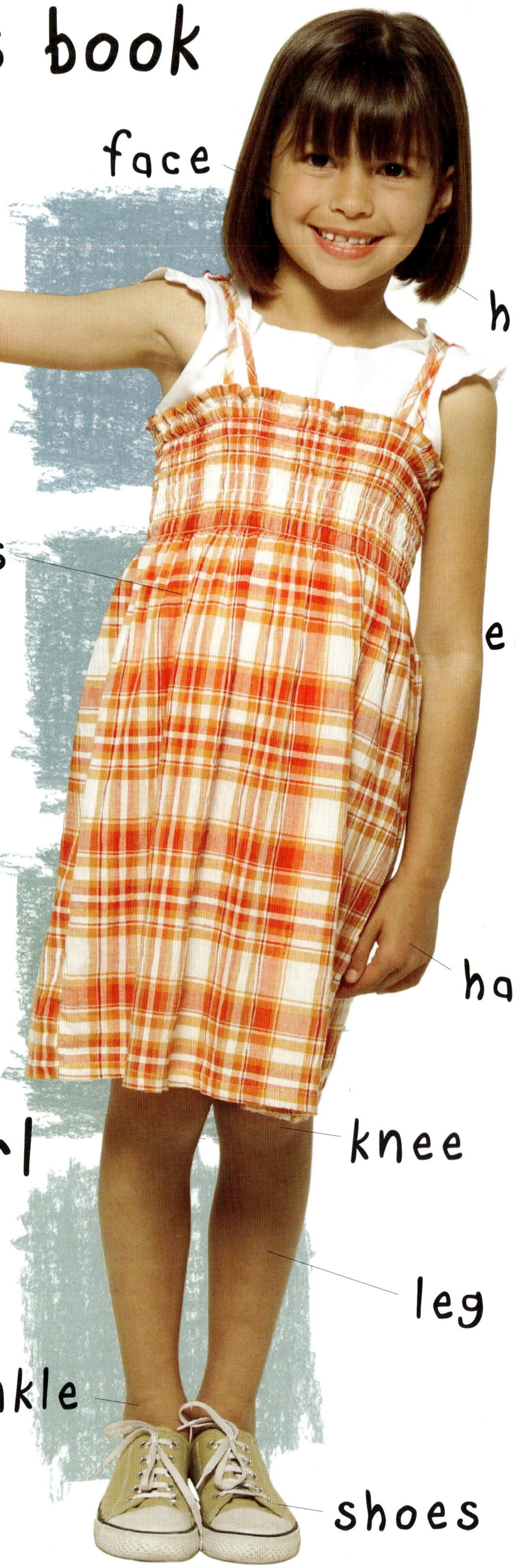
face
arm
finger
thumb
hair
dress
elbow
hand
girl
knee
leg
ankle
shoes

Words has been created especially for young children. It will give them a head start in learning vital pre-school skills such as language and number recognition. It includes the words that children are most familiar with by the age of five. Bright, colourful photographs of familiar and unusual objects will help to widen their knowledge of the world around them. Each section has its own theme, to help young children make the connections between words and pictures.

What pattern is the girl's dress?

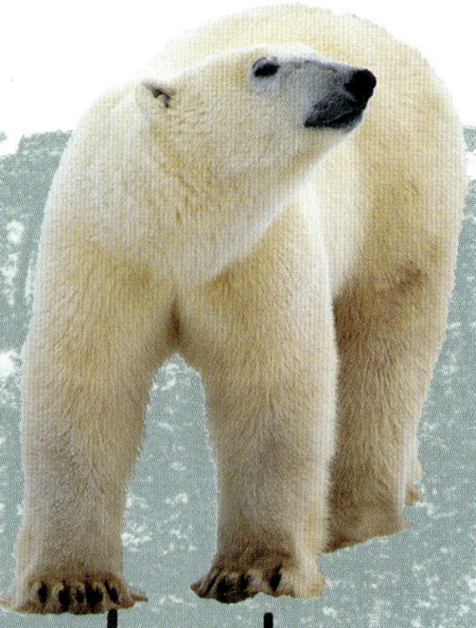
polar bear

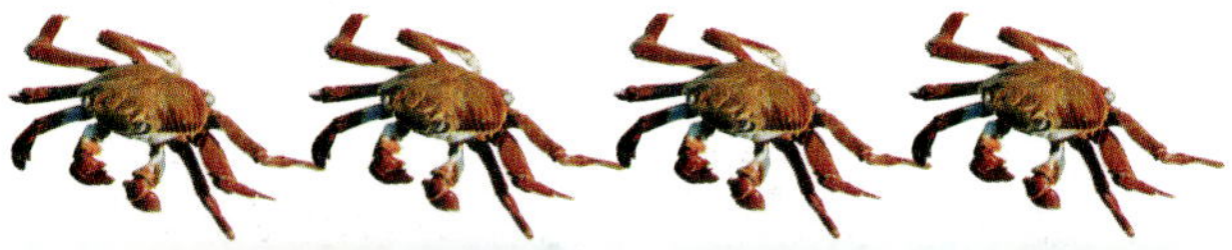

Young children like to look at pictures, and love naming what they see. It is even more fun for them to share a word book with an adult. Start by talking about what is in the picture, and what the object might be used for. Talk about colours and shapes. Look at the scale of the objects – it might be very different on different pages. You can use the questions round the edges of the pages to start a conversation and encourage the child to study the pictures more closely. When they are familiar with the book, show them the index at the back, and explain how it is organised alphabetically.

Children will love searching for the teddy bear on each page.

Where is the letter K?

Can you spell t-o-y?

Alphabet – my letters

What words can you spell using the alphabet?

Can you read all of your letters?

Can you find a Q and an R?

Can you find a V and an F? Can you see all the vowels?

How many letters are in the alphabet?

Nn Oo Pp Qq

Rr Ss Tt Uu

Vv Ww

Xx Yy Zz

Can you point to the letter M?

Can you point to the letter G?

Where is the number 10?

Can you see number 2?

Numbers

Can you count all the way to 32?

Can you point to 10 and 20?

Can you count to 30?

Where is the number 12?

Can you find number 9?

Can you point to all the numbers after 12?

17 seventeen

18 eighteen

19 nineteen

20 twenty

21 twenty-one

22 twenty-two

23 twenty-three

24 twenty-four

25

twenty-five

26

twenty-six

27

twenty-seven

28

twenty-eight

29

twenty-nine

30

thirty

31

thirty-one

32

thirty-two

What number comes after 19?

Can you point to number 21?

Can you see the cone? Where is the cube?

Shapes

Can you draw these shapes?

What colour is the heart shape? How many sides does a pentagon have?

Which bear is stripy?

Patterns

What patterns are the bears wearing?

Colours

Can you see the brushes?
Where is grey?
pen
purple
pink
brown
grey
black
white
brushes
yellow
red
gold
Can you see all the greens?
Can you see all the reds?

Can you see the bumper? Where is the bonnet?

Car

Are the headlights at the front or back of the car?

Where is the steering wheel?

What shape are the wheels?

Can you find the lights?

What colour is the car?

Can you see the windscreen wipers?

Where is the door handle?

What colour is the boy's hair?
Body
face
arm
hand
head
hair
eyebrow
elbow
eye
nose
cheek
chest
ear
mouth
tummy
teeth
hip
lip
chin
leg
neck
knee
foot
1

What do you wear to bed?
What colour is the vest?
Clothes
Which boy has a stripy shirt?
How many children are wearing hats?
What colour is the boy's cap?
vest
pants
pyjamas
slippers
shirt
cap
jumper
bag
jeans
trainers
hat
dress
socks
shoes
shirt
school uniform
shorts

Can you see a cat?

Where is the MP3 player?

The house

Can you find these objects in your own home?

What colour is the telephone?

What time is it on the clock?

Who's on the television?

Which object rings?

How may cushions can you find?

chimney

window

roof

wall

door

garage

gate

radio

houseplant

keys

newspapers

frames

television

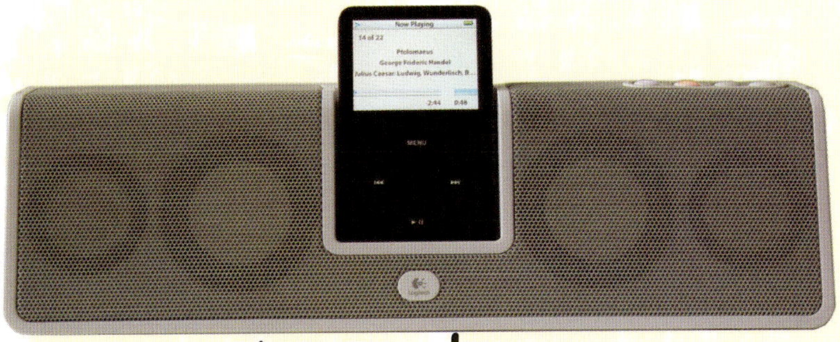

MP3 player

What do you put photographs in?

The garden

Can you find some grass?

Where is the tree house?

Which object would you use to water plants?

Can you point to the birdhouse?

What colour is the rose?

Can you find a trowel?

What colour is the sky?

How many prongs are on the fork?

What colour is the wheelbarrow?

Can you find the soap?

What colour is the sponge?

Good morning

What time do you wake up?

How many toothbrushes can you see?

sun

sponge

shampoo

toilet paper

soap

toothbrush

brushing your teeth

toothpaste

Where is the moon?

What colour is the quilt?

Good night

When do you go to bed?

bed

toilet

pillows

quilt

sleep-over

moon

story book

sleep

teddy

girl

pyjamas

slippers

What do you clean you face with?

What pattern is on the pillows?

Can you find the steak?

Where is the pizza?

What we eat and drink

What is your favourite food?

What colour is the cheese?

Can you find the pancake?

bread
strawberries
steak
scrambled eggs
turkey
salad
Cheese and tomatoes on toast
seafood
pizza
pancake
burger
Can you find the boiled egg?
Can you see the turkey?

Can you point to a son?

Can you see a mother?

Family and friends

How many people are in your family?

Can you see a group of friends?

What colours can you see? Can you find the scissors?

School

What lessons do you take at school?

What can you use to measure things?

What colour is the puppet? Can you find some cards?

Fun and games

What is your favourite game?

Can you find things that bounce?

How many girls are jumping?

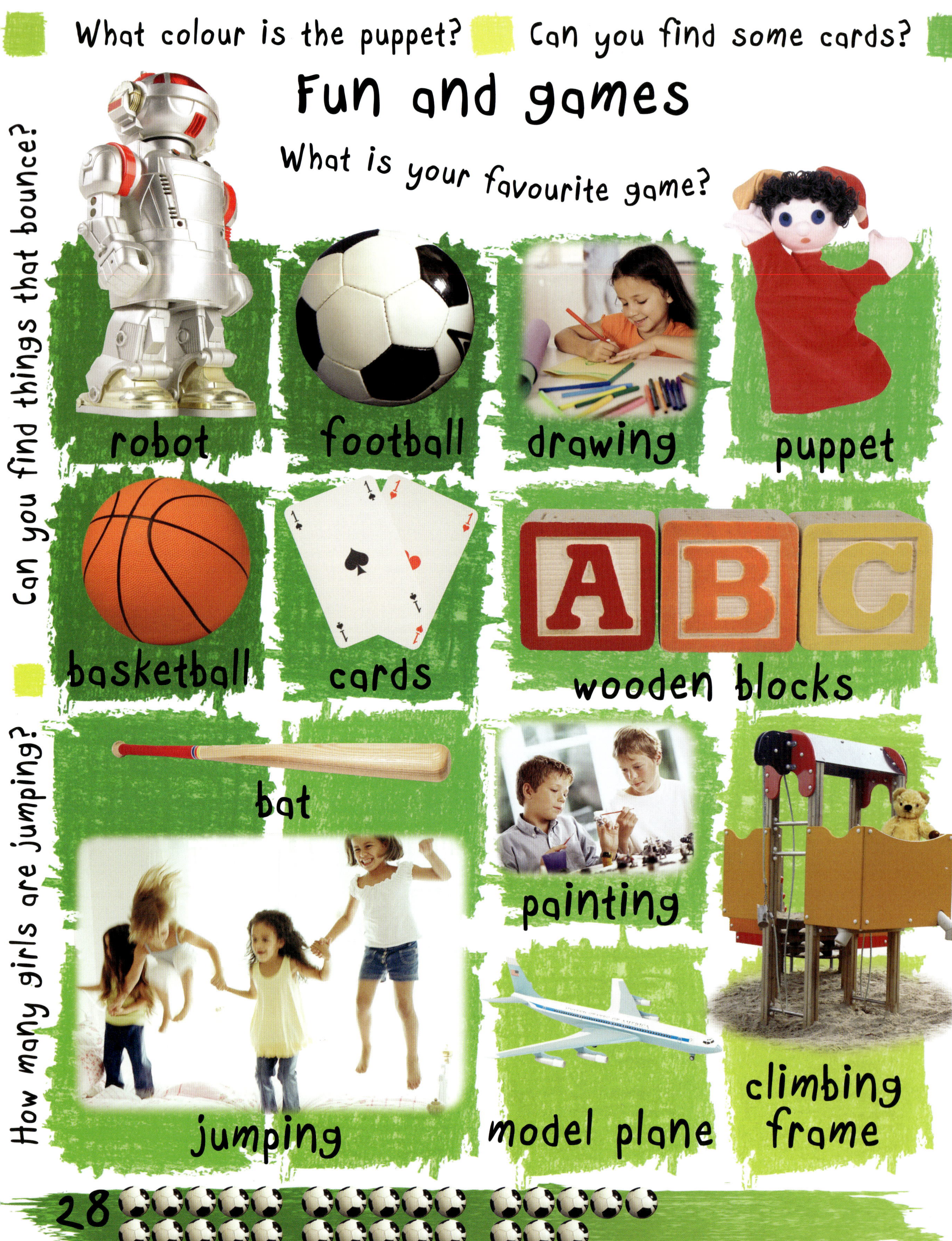

What has three wheels?  What colour is the robot?

How many dolls is the girl holding?

What sports do you like?

chess

bubbles

tricycle

balloon

playing football

playing with dolls

robot car

cuddly toys

Can you see the roadworks? Where are the police?

In the street

What can you find in your street?

What colours are on the traffic light?

street lamp

hydrant

speed camera

telephone box

bin

railings

police

roadworks

recycling bin

statue

traffic light

firemen

cash machine

Where are the firemen?

What colour is the hydrant?

How many different bins can you find?

Can you find the telephone box?

Do you walk on the pavement or in the road?

What colour is the cooker?
Where is the toaster?
In the kitchen
What do you use to stir things?
Can you point to the plates?
tinned food
jug
washing machine
tap
HOT
COLD
egg cup
toaster
bowl
tea towel
fridge
teapot
saucepan
cereal
32

Where is the cereal?
Can you find a kettle?
What can run hot and cold?
What colour is the teapot?
knife and fork
teacup
frying pan
whisk
iron
Can you find a bowl?
cooker
wooden spoon
ice-cream scoop
plates
kettle

Can you find a watermelon?
Where is the orange?
Fruit
Can you point to the pineapple?
Can you see a pear?
Can you see an apple?
bananas
apple
grapes
pineapple
lime
pear
kiwi fruit
lemon
grapefuit
watermelon
peach
orange
tomato
strawberry
cherry
34

Can you see a pepper?
Can you find a turnip?
Vegetables
Can you find the carrots?
cauliflower
onion
broccoli
mushroom
turnip
potatoes
celery
pepper
runner beans
sweetcorn
carrots
radishes
lettuce
Where is the mushroom?
Can you see the potatoes?

Is a cygnet a baby swan?

Where is the fawn?

Baby animals

What is a baby horse called?

What is a baby dog called?

Can you find the bear cub?

kittens

ducklings

foal

calf

piglet

chicks

fawn

puppy

cygnet

lamb

bear cub

Which pet can fly?

What colour is the fish?

Pets

Do you have any pets?

rabbit

dog

guinea pig

washing the dog

fish

cat

parrot

tortoise

Does a tortoise move fast or slowly?

Can you find a cat?

Can you find a shell?

Where is the windmill?

By the sea

What do you use to see underwater?

Can you find a pair of sunglasses?

Can you find a lighthouse?

What can you dig with?

What number can you see on the fishing boat?

shell

crab

surfer

fishing boat

beach

sunglasses

What can you sit on?

Can you find the goose?
What colour is the goat?
How many tractors can you find?
On the farm
How many animals have two legs?
turkey
duck
donkey
wheat
crop
hen
ploughing a field
pig
horse shoe
pony
cow

Can you see the turkey?

Where is the horse shoe?

What colour is the cockerel's tail?

hay bale

sheep

barn

tractor

cockerel

goose

shire horses

goat

milk churn

Can you see the duck?

Can you find 5 hats?

Where are the sandwiches?

Party time

What colours are the balloons?

What colour is the wrapping paper?

Can you find the tart?

Can you spot the clown?

Where are the streamers?

How many orange presents can you spot?

Can you find two red noses?

Can you spot the guitar? Can you find a triangle?

Let's make music!

Which instrument has black and white keys?

Where are the bongos?

Can you see a tambourine?

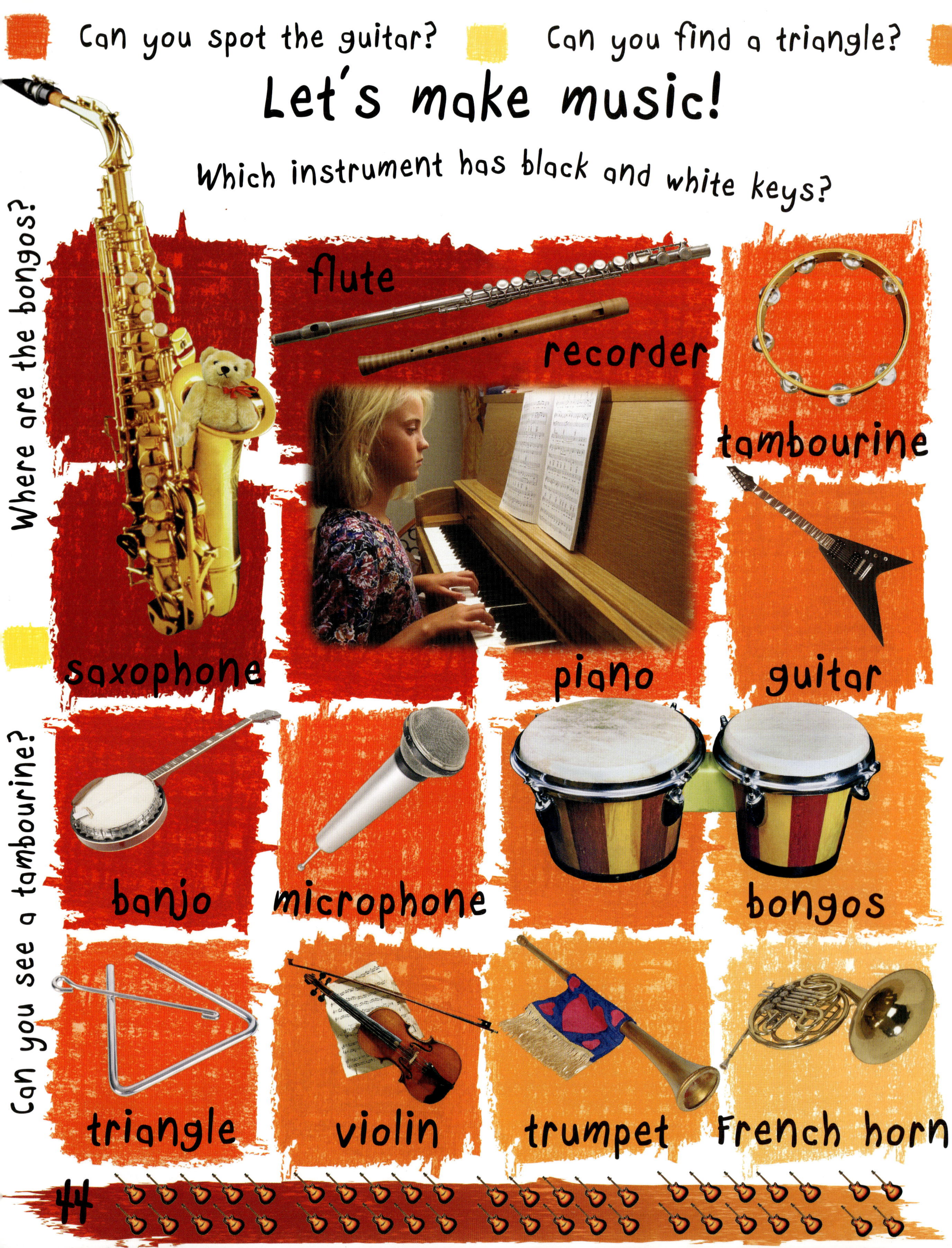

Can you see 2 trombones? Where are the bagpipes?

How many instruments have strings?

bagpipes drum viola trombone

How many drums can you find?

musicians

Can you see the viola?

Where is the zebra?

Can you see an eagle?

Wild animals

How many animals have feathers?

How many animals have stripes?

Can you point to the giraffe?

Where is the camel?

Can you spot the wolf?

Can you see the crocodile?

Which animal has the longest neck?

Can you see a crab?

Can you point to the train? Can you see the plane?

Let's go - on the move!

Which of these vehicles can travel on water?

Where is the skateboard?

Can you see a space shuttle?

What colour is the car?
Which vehicle travels on snow?
Can you point to the boat?
space shuttle
lorry
bus
tram
bicycle
scooter
car
helicopter

Minibeasts

Can you point to a hoverfly?
Can you find the beetle?
How many ants can you spot?
Can you find a grasshopper?
Which animals are slow?
beetle
spider
frog
moth
fly
caterpillar
worm
ladybird
bee
lizard

Where is the worm?

Can you find the butterfly?

Where are the 2 different spiders?

Can you see the caterpillar?

butterfly

snail

hoverfly

scorpion

ant

slug

wasps

grasshopper

Can you see the frog?

centipede

tarantula

dragonfly

What colour is the whale?

Where is the tree?

I am big!

Can you find a yellow digger?

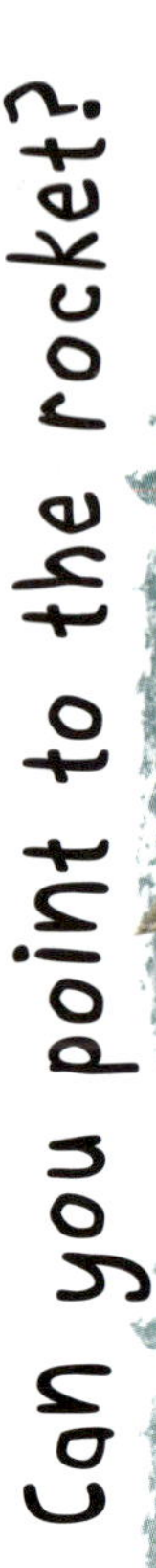

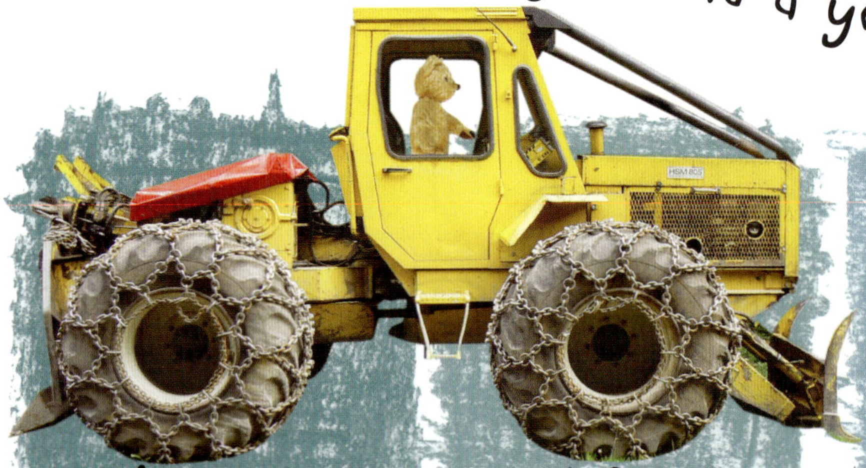

logging machine

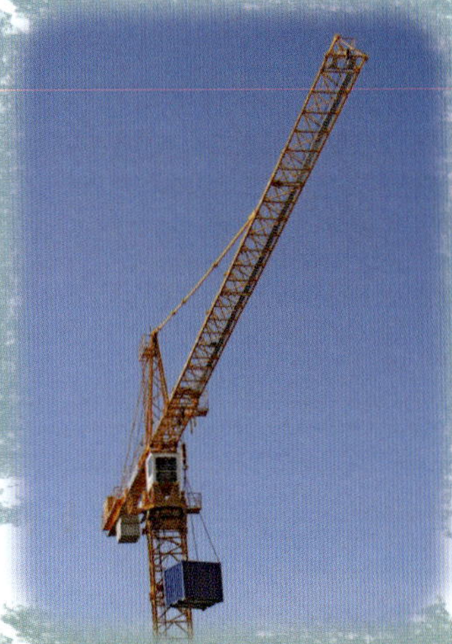

crane

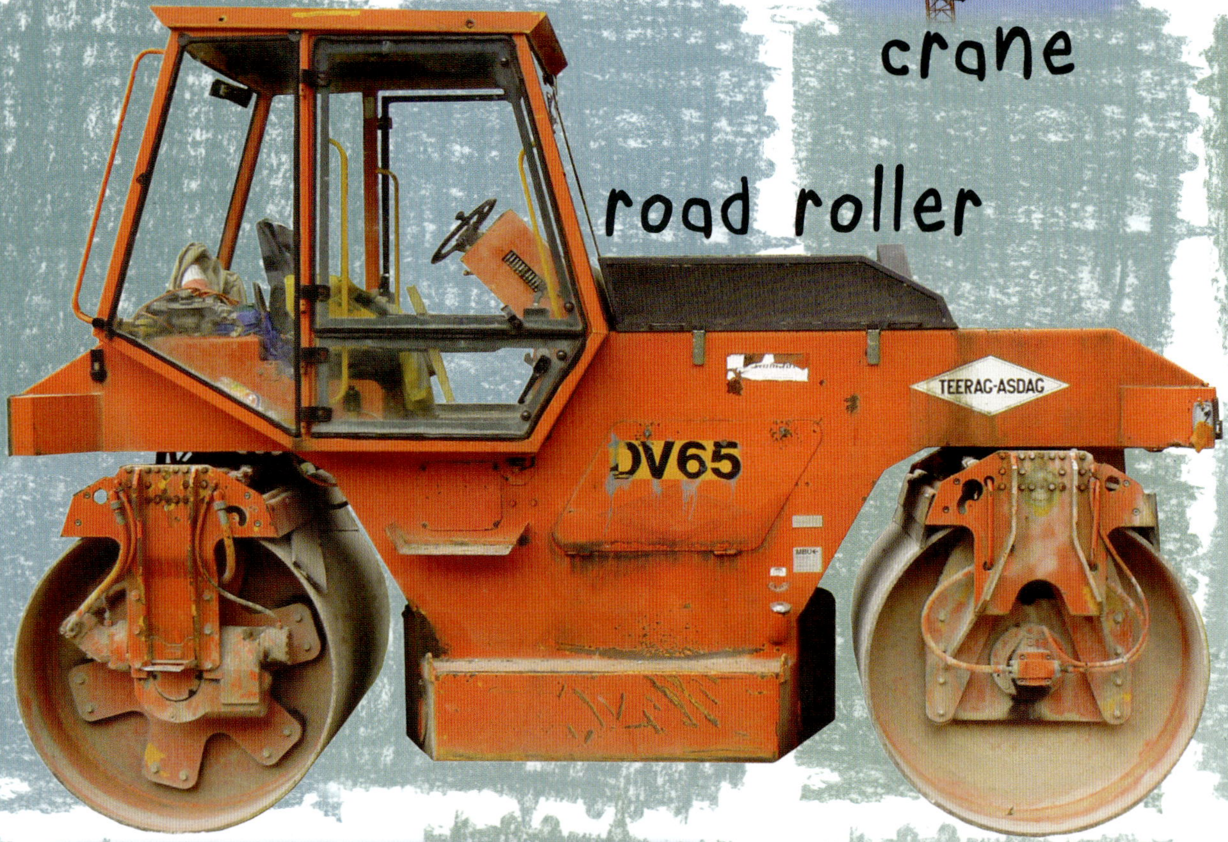

road roller

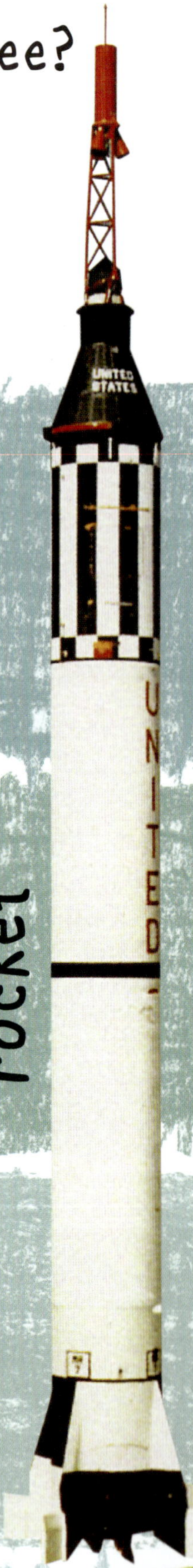

rocket

Can you see an iceberg?

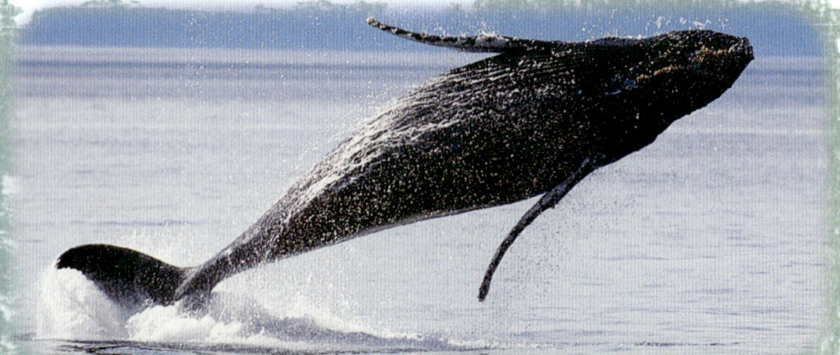

blue whale

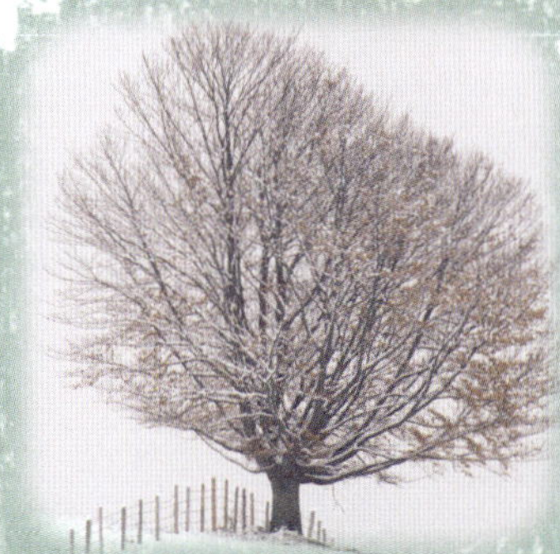

tree

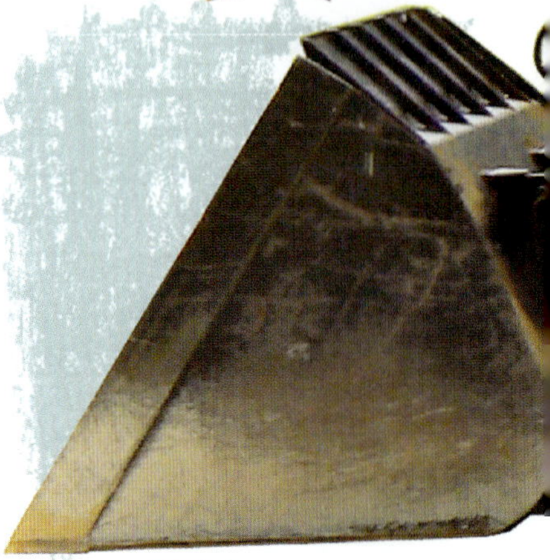

What has big ears?

Can you see the bison?

Where is the logging machine?

castle

bison

cargo ship

elephant

airliner

iceberg

digger

Where is the cargo ship?

Can you find the road roller?

Can you find the art shop? Where can you buy fish?

Shopping

How many men are having haircuts?

Can you see the supermarket?

cake shop

sweet shop

supermarket

art shop

cheese shop

barber shop

fabric shop

fish shop

Where can you buy flowers?

delicatessen

flower shop

toy shop

music shop

dress shop

Which shop sells cheese?

Where is the sweet shop?

Can you point to the oranges?

Can you spot the dress shop?

greengrocer's shop

Can you find the hammer?

Where is the paint brush?

In the workshop

What colour is the oil can?

screwdriver

pruners

paint brush

wrench

pliers

tape measure

oil can

plane

nut

bolt

trowel

workshop

Where might you keep your tools?

Where are the nut and bolt?

Can you see the wrench? Can you point to the plane?

Are there 8 spanners in the set?

Can you spot the screwdriver?

Where is the vice?

Can you point to the lake?

Spot the mountain

Out and about

Where would you go to catch a plane?

Where might you find lots of buildings?

Can you find 2 bridges?

Can you find the canal?

Can you spot 2 rivers?

Where might you find lots of boats?

Point to the waterfall

motorway

canal

airport

buildings

train station

lake

harbour

Where is the city?

Where is the flood?
Can you see the fog?
Weather
Can you see the lightning?
Where is the tornado?
umbrella
hurricane
snow
raincoat
tornado
lightning
flood
Can you spot the rainbow?
rainbow
fog

When will it snow? When do the leaves turn orange?

Seasons

Which season is the coldest?

When is the sky blue?

spring

summer

What follows winter?

autumn

winter

When is play time?

What time is tea time?

Time

How many hours are there in a day?

What time is lunch?

When is home time?

Can you find 'lime'? Can you see 'bananas'?

Index

How many words start with the letter E?

How many words start with K?

Can you find 'envelope'?

Can you find 'whisk'? Can you see 'ship'?

How many words start with Q?

Can you find four words starting with V?

Can you find trumpet?

Index

O

P

Q

R

S

T

U

V

W

Y

Z

Created, designed and edited by:
Elizabeth Branch
Stephen Haynes
David Stewart
Rob Walker
Mark Williams

ISBN-13: 978-1-905638-65-9 (HB)
ISBN-13: 978-1-905638-66-6 (PB)

Published in Great Britain 2007 by Scribblers, a division of Book House, 25 Marlborough Place, Brighton BN1 1UB

Telephone: 01273 603306
Facsimile: 01273 621619

A CIP catalogue record for this book is available from the British Library.

Printed and bound in China.

1 3 5 7 9 8 6 4 2

Photo credits: Banana Stock Ltd, Brand X Pictures, Corbis, Digital Stock Corporation, Digital Vision, Ingram Publishing, John Foxx Images, Jonathan Salariya, Photodisc, Power Photos

Printed on paper from sustainable sources.

www.scribblersbooks.com